MAXIMUM ME

MAXIMUM ME

Your formula for achieving maximum success.

Maxwell R. Jones

Maximum Me

The advice and strategies found within may not be suitable for every situation. This work is sold with the understanding that neither the author nor the publisher are held responsible for the results accrued from the advice in this book.

Although each of the chapters in this book remains factual, some names have been changed to protect the identity and privacy of their families.

Some of the stories included in this book are a work of fiction. Any resemblance to actual persons, living or dead, business establishments, events or locales is entirely coincidental.

All biblical verses and stories are taken from the King James Version (KJV).

For information on licensing and special sales, please contact Maxwell R. Jones at maxwellrjones1@gmail.com

Library of Congress Control Number: 1-9929391611

Trade Paperback ISBN: 978-976-96496-0-6

Hardcover ISBN: 978-976-96496-1-3

Table of Contents

(Belief, Vision, Attitude) + (Performance) = (Results)

Faith + Works = Success

Foreword

Belief

"What does belief mean to me?

Belief is the concept, motivation, philosophy, or thought forming the basis or source of our decisions, values, attitudes, and contributions. It shapes our destiny, legacy, and traditions. Intrinsic values, assumptions, and hope are directly affixed to our belief. Dreams, confidence, and determination propel us forward when we are driven by belief. Faith to "stand up" and be "counted on" cements our belief. More than systems or imagination, belief gives credibility to our creative abilities."

Bishop Ghaly Swann, M. Div., M.A.R

Pastor and Director of Leadership Development & Training

Church of God of Prophecy

Bahamas

Vision

"The Creator has placed in us the innate desire to see things that are not as though they are. Your vision is the key to fulfilling your personal destiny."

H.E. Dr. Kevin C. King

Leader

Kingdom Government Movement (KGM)

The Bahamas

Attitude

"Having a positive attitude evokes the presence and favor of God over one's life journey. It is evident by self-motivation, inspiration, determination, perseverance, and the ability to aspire and propel others into their pre-destined destination. A negative attitude will demolish kingdoms, dethrone kings, impede and destroy families and healthy thriving relationships."

Rosemary Braynen

Registered Nurse

Florida

United States of America

Performance

"'Faith without works is dead.'

As a life coach, using the *Maximum Me* belief principles with my clients is easy and simple as it takes a holistic approach to performance being the action behind your vision. Understanding that work is time, effort, and action, performance is meeting the goals and objectives set out by the vision in a sustainable way. Performance is showing up, being present, putting in the work, taking responsibility for actions and outcomes, setting milestones along the way, and constantly checking to see if you are on course with the vision.

You can never expect to succeed if you do not put in the work; you have to PERFORM!"

Allison A. Levarity

Executive Leader & Life Coach

Grand Bahama, Bahamas

Results

"The success and results attained over my basketball career as a coach can be attributed to the belief that we would be successful. I envisioned that success, and it kept us focused. Despite many setbacks, we maintained a never-give-up attitude. Through hard work, dedication, sacrifice, and love for the game, we became champions. This formula provided me with the best results in becoming the most successful and winningest coach in the New Providence Basketball Association history."

Perry A. Thompson Sr.

Sr. Head Coach

Giants Basketball Club

Nassau, Bahamas

"Life was designed to say "yes" to all of your dreams."

Preface

July 1964

Bernice cried out as the pain of childbirth encircled her like a vicious boa constrictor.

"Push!" the midwife exclaimed. She patted Bernice's wet forehead.

"One more time, Bernice," Dr. Johnson encouraged.

"You can do this," the midwife said. "Give it one more try."

"I'm trying!" Bernice replied through clenched teeth. Bernice gritted her teeth and pushed as hard as she could. Suddenly relief washed over her as the fruit of her labor spilled onto the birthing table.

"A boy," the doctor announced.

Bernice beamed proudly.

"What will you call him?" the midwife asked kindly.

"Maxwell," she replied. "Maxwell Ricardo Jones," She smiled again. She could see the medical team murmuring to each other. They worked diligently with bent heads, as if examining a science exhibit. She watched as they left the delivery room with her newborn baby.

Four hours passed, and Bernice began to feel uneasy. Just as she was about to investigate, the doctor returned. His expression was grave. “Is something wrong?” she asked. She shifted in the bed, still stiff from childbirth.

“Ma’am, your baby was born with a rare respiratory condition. We have discovered that there is a severe issue with the inner lining of his lungs. I’m sorry this has happened to your baby.”

Bernice looked calmly at him as she held onto her squirming, screaming child. “What does this mean? His lungs sound fine to me. Are you sure, doctor?” she asked. She had to elevate her voice above the loud wails.

“He is in a lot of pain,” the doctor replied.

“How can we fix this?” Bernice asked.

“We can give him something to help with the pain but, there is no cure for his condition. He probably won’t live past age sixteen. Take your son home and enjoy the little time you have with him.” He scribbled his notes into the thin, narrow file.

The newborn’s death sentence was delivered, plastered across the page and etched into that moment in history. He was to be executed by a fatal condition that was ruthlessly aggressive and hostile. He now lay squirming in his mother’s arms, sentenced to die at sixteen.

July 1964

That night, Bernice waged war on the prognosis that had been given to her newborn. “Thank you for coming, ladies,” said Bernice quietly.

“He’s beautiful,” Helen cooed as she smiled at the baby.

“Tell us exactly what the doctor said.” Victoria said.

Bernice grimaced as she recollected the doctor's exact words. "They say he won't live past age sixteen. There is something wrong with his lungs." She was quiet but remained strong. "I'm asking the church to go to war with me on this one. The Bible says to pray without ceasing. Every Saturday I will approach the throne of heaven. I will go to war in prayer. Would you ladies stand in agreement and fight with me?"

"Yes," replied Julia. "We will stand in agreement and fight in prayer alongside you."

"I agree," said Sister Roslyn.

"I also agree," said Myrtis.

"I agree," echoed Helen, and Victoria.

"Let's hold hands and form the circle of prayer. Bernice, you sit in the middle with your little one," Sister Roslyn said.

"Thank you. I am forever grateful," Bernice replied. She bowed her head and raised her petition.

One by one they each expressed their deepest, sincerest request, on behalf of the helpless baby who had been dismissed by science and left for dead.

Dear Reader,

If you are reading this, it means you have embarked upon the journey of *Maximum Me*. The two entries above are a reflection of my beginning. Tragic, right? My mother Bernice Jones and many prayer warriors dedicated eighteen years of prayer to my unfortunate circumstance. For eighteen years Helen Dean, Victoria Palmer, Julia Grant, Sister Roslyn "Baby" Capron, and Sister Myrtis Hamilton showed up and went to war in prayer around six o'clock every Saturday evening. Only an emergency caused one of these ladies to miss a meeting.

At these meetings a prayer circle was formed around me, and the prayers of these five women and other church members were raised unto God, pleading that I overcome the fate given to me by the medical team at birth. They believed I would eventually be healthy and prayed without ceasing all the while holding on to the vision that I would be healed. They faithfully showed up every Saturday evening on my behalf. Here I am today significantly beyond the sixteen years placed on my life — the result of the prayers of five women and many others.

There is a God seated on the throne of heaven. I am grateful that I am able to share my story and encourage you to never give up no matter what circumstance you face. You may think that because you are at a disadvantage or simply because the odds aren't in your favor that you have already lost. My friend, I am living proof that the battle is already won. It was won before your entrance into this world.

Today I stand before you, the death sentence placed on me at birth null and void — its invalidation stamped and sealed by The Creator himself. I encourage you to embrace your true purpose that lies within you. May you be empowered to maximize your potential with the utmost confidence in the many possibilities you can achieve. May you be inspired to pursue the most powerful version of you — the maximum you.

Keep fighting,

Maxwell R. Jones

Introduction

"Ricky!" my mom called out to me as I elbowed my way noisily through the door.

"Achoo!" I sneezed loudly before blowing my nose into the dampened tissue that was filled with today's mucus.

"Are you okay?" she asked. Frowning, I looked at her as she bustled around the kitchen.

"The air conditioner at the office made me really sick," I replied. "I don't think I can continue. My supervisor said that I cannot miss more than ten days."

My mom sighed heavily before cleaning her hands with her apron. "Hurry, Helen and the other ladies will be here at any moment to pray for you," she said.

"Okay," I replied. I blew my nose again.

The next thirty minutes flew by. The knock on the door, the greetings, and the prayer circle around me all seemed to pass like a blur. "He's sick again," my mom said. "This new job requires that he works in an air conditioned office space." Sister Helen Dean, Sister Victoria Palmer, Sister Julia Grant, Sister Roslyn "Baby" Capron, and Sister Myrtis Hamilton were the faithful five who showed up almost every Saturday evening. Now, they each prayed once again on my behalf. At that moment, a powerful force moved within me. My mom placed a hand on my shoulder. "Ricky, you don't have to worry about that one anymore." She smiled at me.

Since the events of this day, I have never taken a sick day related to the illness I was diagnosed with at birth. I have concluded that what I felt was God's hand of anointing and the answer to the prayers of the many prayer warriors who had prayed without ceasing for eighteen years. My family and I are forever grateful to the many who showed up for war every Saturday, to go to battle with raised voices and a single and sincere petition — that I be made whole. We may not have had a luxurious lifestyle, but we did have a praying mother who served a powerful God. Over time it became evident that he was all we needed for we possessed good health, food, and a comfortable home.

We had found heaven smack in the middle of one of the settlement of Seagrape in Eight-Mile Rock. Despite the wooden homes and tiny porches, the small village of Seagrape offered something that no family should ever lack — contentment. The three-bedroom, one-bathroom home I shared with my parents and nine siblings not only provided adequate shelter, but it was also the place where vital principles and values were taught daily. I am the son of Johnny and Bernice Jones, the taxi driver and the straw vendor. In our version of paradise, we attended the Pentecostal Church weekly. We attended church at least three to four times every Sunday and the weekly youth meeting every Tuesday. We were encouraged to pay attention throughout the service. This standard was important to my exceptionally religious family and was upheld as a top priority.

There are many moments of my childhood that make me smile as I recall them. Memories like cleaning my father's taxi daily and making straw baskets, which became a specialty of mine. Cleanliness was vital to the taxi industry because it was a reflection of top notch customer service. After hours of weaving and braiding, it felt amazing whenever a client purchased a straw basket or straw hat. We were the first in our settlement to own a

VCR. I can still recall the excitement of that moment and how strict my mom was about adhering to shows suitable for children. Our mom insisted strong moral values be sustained. These moments may seem trivial to some, but they taught me the importance of customer service, diligence, hard work, and integrity. These memorable moments formed the foundation of my character.

The special bond my family shared was rare and unique. Five boys sharing one bed may seem bizarre but, to be honest, we barely noticed. We were so happy and so full of gratitude. We did not have much, but we had each other. The hand-me-down clothing, the worn shoes, the walk to the neighborhood's water pump are all a part of my humble beginning — one that I will forever be proud of.

In October 1981, my older sister Annie "Lean" Charlton, who had kept her eyes peeled for a career opportunity for me, informed me of an opening at a major financial institution, The Commonwealth Bank Ltd. In fact, she got me out of my construction job and took me to complete the application process at the bank. When I landed the job, my family was extremely proud of me. It was a major accomplishment. I was the first banker in the family and in Sea-grape — an achievement that was second to none at the time. I represented a beacon of hope for my family and others in my underprivileged neighborhood. I did not realize how true this was until an event that I will never forget unfolded, one that signifies the beginning of my journey and marked the commencement of a new dawn.

It was a still night; I had just left a celebration party with my childhood friend. This was my first time drinking, and I was drunk. It was the first time I had messed with alcohol. To this day, I do not remember this night, only what my good friend Okell Williams recounted to me. He was my best friend. I had borrowed the family car and had gotten so drunk that he had to drive me home.

Now, as we pulled up to my house, Bagsy was under the lamp pole near the trash bins shooting dice and drinking. This is not his real name, but for the purpose of this book, I'll call him Bagsy. You might be wondering, who is Bagsy? He was better known as the homeless guy. Bagsy was frequently seen here and there begging for money or food. He could often be found just lying around. Ironically, he was a heavy drinker who was well known in the community and, as luck would have it, he was sober enough to help me out of the car, up the walkway, and into my home. The drunk helping the drunk. Ironic, right? Even more strange, he was helping out the son of two dutiful and very religious citizens who was highly respected in the community. Who would have thought? My tie and work clothing were rumpled and my shoes were in my hands. I was in bad shape. Yes, a barefoot Maxwell Ricky Jones the banker stumbled up the Jones' walkway, on the verge of blacking out. Well, this is what they tell me. As I said before, to this day I do not remember the events of that night.

The next morning, there was a knock at the door. My mother got up and placed the straw basket she had been weaving on the table. "I wonder who it is," she said as she tied her apron strings tighter. "Ricky, would you see if there is more macaroni left?" she pointed to kitchen. "Maybe someone needs more food." She seemed tired today, but she opened the door with enthusiasm. "Hi Bagsy, how can I help?" she said pulling her apron strings tighter around her. "Are you hungry?" She smiled at him.

I curiously peeked out from behind the cabinet. An awkward Bagsy looked back at me.

"Good day, Ms. Bernice," he said in a low voice. "I need to talk to Ricky."

My mom's face turned. The condescending look she wore should have sent Bagsy on his way; however, he remained true to his mission of needing to speak to me.

"Ms. Bernice, I really need to talk to Ricky," he said.

My mother was uncertain what this all meant. She wondered, what did Bagsy want with her son? What did he want with the son who had just landed himself the job of the century? She was astounded by his request, but something in Bagsy's voice seemed sincere. Strangely she felt his sincerity in that moment and granted his appeal. "Ricky!" she called in an unsure voice.

I came to the front door, and Bagsy took me aside into the privacy of the backyard under the tree and what followed is what I consider to be the event that is one of the most impactful occurrences of my life. It forged a fork in the road for me, one that was to determine my rise or fall.

"Man, Ricky, what I saw last night …" he began. "I was too ashamed and embarrassed!" "Last night, you was drunk, drunk and I had to carry you to your door. Promise me I ain ga ever see you like dat again."

I blinked at him, overwhelmed with humiliation. Here was Bagsy, of all people, scolding *me*! He was giving advice out of a genuine desire to help. He seemed so sincere that I perked up and took into account everything he was saying to me.

"You see me here," he said. "I know dat I is a joonser and I know dat I ain ga amount to anything. But, we looking fa you ta make it out of dis community, so dat you can give da younger ones some hope!" he said. "We counting on you ta make something of yourself! We're hoping dat you become da bank manager someday, so dat others can see dat it is possible for a poor boy from a poor community! Promise me that you ain ga ever drink like dat no more," he continued. "Don't do dat again! Bring me da drink next time."

I was silent, but his words pierced me, leading to the realization that a community — my community — was counting on me! Even Bagsy was counting on me! What he told me made sense. I had a major responsibility to uphold.

I easily lose control at the smallest amount of liquor. Some may be able to maintain control when they drink, but I have come to the realization that I am irresponsible when it comes to drinking alcohol. That night has proven this. Alcohol clouds my judgment. Knowing this, I have decided to stay away from it. It is said that alcohol limits the ability to function properly and encourages the lack of judgment in some people. I experienced this firsthand when I decided to drink that night. I'm not bashing alcohol. I simply came to the understanding that alcohol could destroy any future potential I possessed. This is a principle I have decided to live by because of the negative effect alcohol has on me. I wasn't prepared to let down my family, friends, even more so my community. I decided to embrace my potential from that day forward. That day I made up my mind that I would never get drunk again. Bagsy's speech was one to be remembered.

Today, I am exactly who Bagsy believed I could be. He believed in me and was able to convince me to believe in myself. This belief enabled Bagsy to generate a vision for me. After Bagsy's heartfelt advice, that belief and vision were transferred to me, causing me to decide to have the right attitude which led to me giving the right performance that led to dynamic results.

Today, I am the Vice President of Accounts Control and Collection at Commonwealth Bank Ltd. Through hard work and dedication, I have achieved what Bagsy saw in me and have excelled even beyond the branch manager post that he saw. There are times when our greatest blessing comes from the most unlikely of places. It is a reminder to never judge the messenger but to concentrate on the message. The message that had the greatest impact on my life came from someone deemed unworthy. It was through that conversation with Bagsy that I acquired a desire to straighten up and fly right. I am humbled that my life, my goals, and my achievements have empowered my community and even beyond this will hopefully empower many generations to come. And this was all strengthened by Bagsy's belief in me. It was because of that conversation that I decided to walk in my purpose and chase my dreams.

Now, chasing a dream takes guts. It takes hard work. Some dreams are terrifying, while others may seem downright unattainable. Maybe you want to pursue medical school, or perhaps you want to attain that promotion at work. Maybe you want to start your very own business, or possibly save a down payment for a new home. You begin to actively pursue your dream and halfway through, you become overwhelmed by the process, your hopes get dampened, and eventually you call it quits. Sound familiar? Many have experienced this unfortunate series of events — the process of your goal being at the tips of your fingers only to give up before ever grabbing hold of it. Countless individuals give up before ever fully achieving what they set out to do. But what if I told you, life was designed to say "yes" to all of your dreams? What if I told you that no mountain is impossible to climb, and with the correct implementation of the formula discussed in this book, you can achieve all of your dreams? The first three principles — belief, vision, and attitude — embody mindset. These are equivalent to faith. The principle of performance embodies action. This principle is equivalent to works.

(Belief, Vision, Attitude) + (Performance) = (Results)

Faith + Works = Success

This highly effective formula that consists of five parts helps you to accompany your goal from start to finish. It allows you to set the bar, meet, and, in some cases, even exceed all expectations, and see your goals through to the very end. The journey of attaining a goal may be long and tiring; however, it is when you unleash the power of the formula discussed in this book, you become unstoppable, relentless, and in command of the "yes" life has to offer. When you master the art of this formula, you master the art of achievement, and you can dominate in life and business. The internalization of the *Maximum Me* formula is a fundamental necessity regarding achievement and success. Program your mind to master this formula, and it will significantly help you in successfully achieving your goals.

For example, if your dream is to become a doctor, you must see yourself as a doctor during your journey through medical school. Your belief that you will eventually become a doctor carries you through. Now, the process of medical school can be overwhelming; however, you will be dedicated to spending endless nights studying and many long hours in the laboratory and be extremely committed to a demanding and tiring schedule. Why? Because you believe you will become a doctor. This commitment then leads to excellent examination results and high test scores. Therefore, at the end of your medical school journey, you will receive your medical degree! Your belief that you will become a doctor kept you motivated throughout your journey. You remained grounded in your decision and saw your goal through to the very end. Your **belief** of becoming a doctor led to your **vision** of seeing yourself as a doctor, which led to an **attitude** of remaining committed to long hours of studying, leading to **performing** at a level that delivered excellent **results** on examinations and tests, which eventually led to the achievement of your goal — a medical degree!

Your belief system affects your vision — how you see things. Your vision affects your attitude — how you approach things. Your attitude affects your performance — how well you execute that thing. Your performance determines the level of your success, or the level of your results. Remember, life is designed to say "yes" to all of your dreams. It is my hope that at the end of this book, you will be inspired to hunt down your dreams, chase them, and conquer each goal you set for yourself. May this book encourage you to demonstrate tenacity and intensity toward your aspirations and goals. No matter how big that dream may be or how big that vision may seem, hold on to it. Keep fighting! Keep pushing. Don't throw in the towel too soon.

Life is like a series of doors. Some stop knocking at door number three, not realizing that the answer to their goal is just behind door number four. Many give up too early and never experience the "yes" life has to offer. You must first believe that life was indeed designed to say "yes" to all of your dreams. Believe that no matter how many times someone tells you "no," you will eventually receive a "yes." Your dreams and goals will be rejected by many. There will be times you want to quit and give up on your ventures simply because they *seem* impossible. Many have had big dreams but gave up too soon. Don't give up no matter how bad things may seem. Everything you need to succeed has already been provided. It's almost like a puzzle: the pieces all exist, and you just have to find the pieces and assemble them in order to complete the larger picture. Your dreams deserve to be given a chance. Keep digging until you arrive at the moment your dream takes flight. Ignore the rejection you will encounter until the moment it soars.

The dynamics of the Creator and earth's creation has always astounded me. In the first five days, the Creator formed the sun, moon, stars, plants, trees, sea creatures, and birds of the sky. On the sixth day, he created the creatures of the earth. Then he created man. He saved man for last. Everything else was placed into the earth first. Every provision man would have needed was designed first. It was designed for him to be successful. Life was designed that if you walk in your purpose, you will be successful. You were created for a great purpose. The Creator designed you with a specific purpose that only you can fulfill. For example, a soap manufacturer creates his product and sends it out to stores with the confidence it will perform the way it is meant to perform. It is the same with you. You were sent with a purpose inside you.

Your purpose lies in that great thing you are meant to do. Your destiny is positioned at the end of that great thing you are meant to achieve. With hard work and determination, you are predestined to arrive at your destination. A magnetic pull exists between your purpose and your destiny. This magnetic pull is your passion. Your journey is the space in between your purpose and your destiny.

Faith plays a huge role also. It is a navigation system that propels you toward your destination. It acts in the same way a GPS tracker tracks a destination. It is that inner voice that tells you whether to go left, right, or straight ahead. It guides you as to how to get to your destiny. It is important to mention that even if you miss a turn you will still reach your destination. Just as a GPS tracker recalculates and redirects you, your faith will also steer you back on the right path toward your destiny. Have faith in your purpose even if you don't fully understand it yet. The important thing to remember is to get started. Keep walking. Sooner or later you will feel the vibration. Sooner or later that magnetic pull will get stronger and stronger until you have reached your destination. By doing this you are truly embracing your purpose.

On your journey you will eventually gain momentum. The closer you get to your destiny the stronger that magnetic pull will be. Do not worry if you're not sure what your purpose is. Some people find out very early, some find out very late, some accidentally, and some people are thrust into it. Some may have been walking in it for a while but have not fully realized it as yet. Even if you don't have a clear understanding of what it is yet, here is one thing that is certain, even if you do not know what your purpose is, you are certain of what it isn't. How many times do you hear of students who go to college to major in a specific field and then later change their major to something else?

Remember your steppingstone to your purpose and destiny can be in all different arenas, but it will all work together for your good. I used to be a busboy many years ago. This taught me how to serve. At present my arena is in banking. The experience of being a busboy prepared me for the banking arena. Today I make every effort to serve my clients with the same excellent customer service skills that I learned as a busboy. You may not know exactly what it is now, but at some point in time there will be an inner passion that will draw you toward your purpose. One thing that will help you to identify your purpose is to ask yourself, "Do I love this even beyond the pay?" Money will not be the driving factor behind it. Are you doing it for the compensation of inner fulfillment and satisfaction? Another indication will be whether you are getting progressively good at it. This realization of purpose can come at any age. Embrace that thing you are meant to do no matter what age you are.

You must do what you were created to do because you were intended to be successful at it. Don't underestimate your purpose. Don't compare it to anyone else's. You must see the value in that great thing that only you can birth. The heavens have set everything in place for you to succeed. Don't worry if you don't have the money or simply cannot see how things will work in your favor. With hard work and determination, it will work out. The heavens have supplied you with everything you need to succeed. You will win if you put in the work. It's almost like an entertainment wrestling match. It is fixed, but you still have to fight. Don't get the world's standard of measuring success confused with your purpose. We are all placed here to do something. It can be to lead or to support. Sometimes you are just paving the way for others.

A great example of this is Frank Rutherford, the first Bahamian Track and Field Olympic medalist who won a bronze medal in 1992. According to The Bahamas Olympic Committee, this was a massive accomplishment for The Bahamas (https://www.bahamasolympiccommittee.org/legends). It created a recognition that The Bahamas can indeed compete on a global level in the track and field arena. Some years later, the team of Pauline Davis-Thompson, Debbie Ferguson-McKenzie, Eldece Clarke, Sevatheda Fynes, and Chandra Sturrup, also known as the Golden Girls, became legends and won a gold medal for the 4 x 100 in the year 2000 in Sydney, Australia. The Golden Girls are one of the most accomplished Olympic groups in Bahamian track and field history. Are we to say that Frank Rutherford failed when he did not receive a gold medal? His purpose may have been to inspire The Golden Girls so that they may know that it is possible. Do not think because you are not at the top that you have not achieved your purpose. Sometimes your purpose lies in laying the foundation and inspiring someone else to go even further.

Consider another example. Every character in a movie does not have a leading role. There are some characters who only play a supporting role. Yet, if you take out these supporting characters, the movie is not as dynamic. You may not have a major part, but it does not mean that you are not successful when playing your part and making the entire movie even better. A part of

Frank Rutherford's purpose may have been tied to inspiring other Bahamians to compete on an international level. Sometimes you are called to the world stage. Sometimes you are called to help a community. And, sometimes you are called to help an individual.

Every piece of the puzzle has a purpose working together to achieve a bigger picture. Do not judge the success of the ship with the same criteria you judge the private jet. Each serves its own purpose. The private jet was intended to carry a few passengers in a short amount of time. The ship was designed to carry cargo and freight at a slower pace. Each serves its own purpose. Each was designed with a different intent. It was intended for the private jet to have speed. Also, it was intended for the ship to go at a slower pace. Both serve a great purpose. If the jet arrives at its destination, it has served its purpose. If the ship arrives at its destination, it has also served its purpose. The jet cannot say to the ship, "I am greater than you because I am faster." The ship cannot say to the jet, "I am greater than you because I am bigger." They are both great as long as each achieve its intended purpose. The jet was built for speed and the ship was built for cargo space. The family who owns the jet will be happy as long as they arrive at their destination on time. The family who owns the ship will be happy as long as their cargo arrives at its destination on time. Just as the Creator who designed you will be happy as long as you serve that purpose for which you are intended.

Do not compare your purpose to anyone else's purpose. Do not confuse being great with being famous. Many confuse greatness with the world's standard of greatness. Some may be called to become great athletes. Another may be called to raise the next president. These are both great purposes. Do not underestimate your purpose. Do not feel as though your purpose is less important than another's. You were put on this earth to do a great thing. I want you to achieve this great thing. Greatness is not necessarily tied to fame, but it is tied to legacy.

Legacy goes beyond being famous. For example, there are many exceptional and extraordinary icons who have been adopted as children. These amazing human beings have grown up to play a major part in raising the bar and impacting many generations. Now, a part of their biological mother's great purpose was to give birth and bring each child safely into the world. A part of their adoptive mother's great purpose was to rear them and prepare each child to make their mark on the world. Do not take your purpose lightly even if it is not great according to society's standards. The world recognizes celebrities and fame; however, greatness goes beyond this. Each child's biological mother was the portal that brought them into this world, and so her purpose was a great one. Heaven gave the adoptive mother an impactful human to rear; therefore, her purpose was also a great one. Both women may never be famous, but both served a great and extraordinary purpose.

Sometimes your great purpose lies in helping someone achieve theirs. Service to mankind is still important. It is a great duty. What was Mother Theresa known for? Kindness. She was not rich. She never held a political position, but she still served a great purpose. Don't tie your greatness to how well known you are. Tie your greatness to who you impact. I am not bashing fame because fame may come. There are some great people who are popular on the world's stage. There are some great people who are popular in their arena. And, there are some great people who aren't popular at all. Yet, all three can be great. I challenge you to discover what makes you great by embracing your purpose. May this book inspire you to use our formula and chase your dreams and aspirations with confidence and assurance that it is possible.

The *Maximum Me* formula may seem unusual, but, in time,

you'll see that this formula works in both business and in life. With the adaptation of the *Maximum Me* formula, you are certain to achieve any goal. This formula may seem unrealistic, but in the end, it will be worth it. You must believe that you are beyond capable of achieving the goals you set for yourself. Groundbreaking knowledge is not always easy to receive at first, but, over time, if you examine the dynamics of this formula and test them, you'll discover that they will withstand the test of time. In time, you will see the value they can bring to your journey. Time will prove the *Maximum Me* formula to be valuable on your journey in pursuing excellence. I have confidence that as a result of internalizing each step of this formula, you will become the most powerful version of you. Embodying the most powerful version of you allows you to fully operate within your purpose. I challenge you to adopt the principles that embody this formula and step into the most dynamic version of you — you who stand unchallenged, unrelenting, and filled with confidence when chasing your goals.

"True belief drives action."

CHAPTER ONE

Belief

(Belief, Vision, Attitude) + (Performance) = (Results)

Faith + Works = Success

There is an ancient story about four eastern travelers who journeyed across the desert. It was custom to carry a tent, a rope, a stake, and a camel for the trip. The voyage was long, and it was tradition for the travelers to pitch their tent and tie up the camel so he did not wander away. Now, the youngest and most inexperienced of the travelers had forgotten his rope and his stake. Night came and the three travelers who had their ropes pitched their tents, tied up their camels, and turned in for the night. The young and inexperienced traveler who had forgotten his rope stood outside of his tent holding his camel.

The eldest of the travelers happened to get up in the middle of the night, and asked "What are you doing?"

The young traveler replied, "I have forgotten my rope and if I go to sleep, my camel will run away."

The older traveler then gave him some advice. He ended by assuring the young traveler that if he heeded this advice, in the morning his camel would be right there.

The young man struggled with the advice for a while. He then said to himself, “What have I got to lose?” and went ahead and did exactly what the older traveler had told him to do. He went into his tent and finally fell asleep. The next morning, his camel was standing exactly where he had left him. The young traveler was baffled. You might be wondering, what was the older traveler’s advice? What did he tell the younger traveler to do?

He had said, “Go to the camel and look him in the eyes. Ensure that the camel is able to see your actions clearly. Take an imaginary rope and tie it around the camel’s neck. Make an imaginary knot. Let the camel see you do this. Ensure that the camel sees your every move. Then take an imaginary mallet and nail the imaginary stake into the ground. Take the other end of the imaginary rope and tie it to the imaginary stake. When you do this, the camel will truly believe that he is tied.”

Now the next morning, the other travelers unpitched their tents, untied their camels, and prepared to resume the long journey. The younger traveler unpitched his tent, climbed onto his camel, and nudged him. The camel did not move. The young traveler kicked the camel hard. The camel did not move. Finally losing his temper, the young traveler began to beat the camel.

When the older traveler saw that the young traveler’s beating would kill the camel for sure, he climbed down from his own camel and stopped the young traveler. He looked the young traveler’s camel in the eyes and ensured the camel was able to see his actions. He untied the imaginary rope from around the camel’s neck and picked up the imaginary stake, all the while ensuring the camel saw his every action. It was then the camel finally moved forward.

Was the camel tied? Yes, or no? Let’s think about it. While he may not have been physically tied, he believed he was tied, and as a result of his belief, his behavior was aligned with being physically tied. This is the power of belief. Be careful what you believe because your belief holds power over your actions. You may be hindering yourself from excelling to your highest potential when you believe that someone or something has you tied when in reality you aren't. Although obstacles and circumstances may slow you down for a while, they cannot ultimately stop you.

Many times we stop ourselves or limit ourselves by giving others more power than they actually have over us. The power for you to succeed lies within you. Your boss may determine how far you go in your company or industry; however, your boss cannot determine how far you go nationally. Your prime minister or president may be capable of influencing how far you go nationally, but they cannot determine how far you go in the world. I'm not saying that people aren't powerful, but don't give people power over you when the power lies within you. You hold true power over your dreams, and realizing this helps your dreams to not only survive, but to also thrive. Be careful about what you believe because your beliefs hold power.

The camel in the story did not move because he believed he was tied up. His belief affected his vision, as he saw himself tied to the stake. His vision affected his attitude, and he accepted that it was his fate to remain there until his master released him. His attitude affected his performance — he did nothing. His performance affected his results — he was nearly beaten to death.

What do you believe about your goal? Do you believe in the possibility of its achievement? Do you believe you are capable of going against all odds and achieving what it is you want? Do you believe you can eventually gain that job position you wish to have? Will you apply for medical school, or will you dismiss the idea because you do not have the funds? Will you put yourself out there and start that business, or will you terminate the thought because you do not have the clients yet? True belief drives action. You will either do nothing or you will do something. Believe in your goal. Believe in your dream. Believe that you can achieve what it is you want to achieve. Believe in your capacity to conquer your goal. Why? Because life was designed to say "yes" to all of your dreams. Your dreams can indeed come true.

Many have struggled with the ability to have confidence in something without proof. It's easy to rely on the assurance of a thing rather than in the belief of a thing. Strengthen the muscle of your belief system, and the probability of your achievement will be heightened. As you embrace the pursuit of your dreams and goals, keep in mind that the first principle you need to embody is belief. Belief and core values are often used interchangeably. Most corporations usually use the term core values. Most individuals use the term belief. The principle of belief represents the first step in getting what it is you want to achieve. You can either believe that you can, or you can believe that you can't. The principle of belief sets the tone throughout your journey. It establishes a mental manifestation that causes you to act accordingly. Everything starts with your belief system. Belief is the first principle that kick starts your journey of achievement. How strong or how weak your belief system is, determines the level of success you will achieve. You must realize that you were born for a specific purpose.

The ability to have a mental representation of how a situation will turn out despite your present circumstances is hard, but it is necessary. Each principle in the *Maximum Me* formula are needed to work together to achieve success. Don't focus on one. Just as each part of a machine is needed to operate, all parts of this formula are needed to function. However, belief is the foundation; it's the underlying basis of your journey to success. Keep belief alive and you will keep hope alive. Belief is the generator that empowers your journey and boosts your assurance. It causes a surge of confidence to empower your thoughts and keeps you focused on your goal. Your success is tied to the power of your belief. It is essential to have a strong sense of belief in what it is you want to achieve. Ask yourself, why do I want to achieve this? Why should I keep knocking? The sacred significance that lies within your journey is embodied by your belief. Your belief will then serve as an anchor in tough times, preventing you from giving up before you achieve your goal. It keeps you cemented throughout your journey and keeps you aligned with what you are trying to achieve.

True belief influences your behavior. Your belief is a reflection of your state of mind and is often aligned with your actions. It is the driving force behind everything you do, leading up to your achievement. Your actions can be traced back to your core belief. Your belief is the determining factor behind your every action. Your beliefs can change and your beliefs can grow. Before you can act differently, you have to think differently. The book of Proverbs tells us that, "As a man thinketh in his heart, so is he." Here is a simple analogy: If the airport is your destination and you believe the airport is west, in which direction will you go? If you truly believe it is west, you will not go in an eastern direction because it is not aligned with your belief. You act according to what you believe. Your belief serves as the basis for your actions. It is the embodiment of the motive for your journey.

Do you believe you hold the capacity to deliver at a caliber that exceeds expectations? Do you believe that the achievement of your goal is possible? Quite often, individuals do not recognize their value and fall short on their achievement due to their lack of belief. It is belief that distinguishes you from others. Belief sets apart the CEO from the line staff. Recognize your value and believe that you can, no matter how big your dream may seem because big dreams require big faith. Hold on firmly to your belief and you will see your goal through to the very end. Hold true to what you believe and you will thrive at every level your journey takes you. Your faith forms an armor that helps you to keep fighting until you have achieved your goal. The fact that you believe is the first step to conquering that dream, that goal that you want to achieve.

A good example of this is the biblical story of David and Goliath. David was a shepherd and the youngest of the eight sons of Jesse from the Israelite tribe of Judah. Goliath was the champion of the Philistine army. No one dared challenge him. That is, no one but David. David stepped into the fighting arena with five stones, a slingshot, and the belief that God would intervene on his behalf. David's stone pierced Goliath's head with such force Goliath fell to the ground dead. Centuries later we are still talking about David and Goliath. David acted according to his faith in God. David took action with one belief in mind, "Goliath, with God's help I am going to slay you." That is exactly what he did. If you believe that you *can't* do something, then you will do nothing. If you believe that you *can* do something, then you will follow through with action. David believed that God would deliver Goliath into his hands, and that is exactly what happened. He defeated Goliath. At the end of it all David was victorious.

Do you really believe what you say you believe? This is a personal question that only you can answer. There are many who abandon their beliefs, values, and principles when they experience financial problems, relationship loss, or fear of losing their life. By no means am I saying that these matters are trivial. These circumstances are serious and will test your core beliefs. What I am talking about is betraying your core belief or set of values. There will be some low points on the road to great success. Despite the risk of death, Dr. Martin Luther King Jr. believed in his dream and was willing to die for it. He worked hard to bring equality to America and guarantee civil rights for all regardless of race. He was well-known for his peaceful approach to protesting and belief that both races could live in harmony. In 1968 he was assassinated. Today his legacy lives on, and his beliefs remembered.

Your core belief assists by giving you integrity and conviction that cannot be bought. The fear of death did not stop Dr. King. Let nothing stand in the way of your beliefs. There is an invisible line that each of us must draw. A line that you will not cross no matter what. A line that says no matter what happens I will not do this. This line looks different for everyone. For me, I will not steal no matter what happens. Why? Because I believe in honesty. Your belief system can be influenced by at least three factors. Believing that you can and believing that you can't can be a result of:

- What you are taught
- Your experiences
- What you observe

Believing you can achieve your goal is connected to the strength of your belief. Believing you can't achieve your goal is also linked to the strength of that belief. Why do individuals believe that they can't? If you uproot this belief, you will find one common denominator — fear. Fear is usually the most prominent reason why an individual believes that he or she cannot attain their goal. Most times, fear can lead to paralysis, hesitation, and doubt. Individuals experience a lack of confidence and an unwillingness to pursue a goal because of fear. They fear failure. In the same way, fear can be used as motivation. There are some individuals who experience a willingness to keep going because they fear failure. These unique and exceptional individuals push beyond the feeling of fear and doubt, in fear of not achieving their goal. Small and large strides are made daily, pushing them in the direction of their goal because they do not want to fail. They fear failure.

I used to think that your fears shaped or had influence over your beliefs, but I have learned over the years that it is the other way around. Believing that you can achieve your goal can outweigh fear. If you believe the negative aspect of a circumstance, this can produce fear. However, belief trumps fear and destroys doubt. If you become convinced and believe the positive in light of the negative, the fear will be swallowed up by the positive belief. I know there are many illustrations one can draw to emphasize this point, but allow me to reference one of the most powerful illustrations of belief conquering fear.

The ancient story is told of how a great storm arose on the open sea of Galilee. This storm was so fierce it caused a group of experienced fishermen to fear greatly for their lives. Just as they were about to perish, the story goes on to say that their Lord Jesus appeared walking on the water. This supernatural act caused the fishermen to become even more fearful. They believed he was a ghost.

Jesus immediately told them not to be afraid.

But as scared as the disciples were, one disciple, Peter, strongly believed that the man walking on the water was indeed his Lord. Peter replied, "Lord, if it is you, tell me to come to you on the water."

Jesus replied, "Come."

Peter got out of the boat and began to walk on the water towards his Lord. However, he lost focus when he saw the wind and waves, and he instantly began to sink. He cried out, "Lord, save me!"

Jesus, who knows that your belief will give you the confidence to do great things, caught the man and said to him, "You of little faith, why did you doubt?"

Peter strongly believed it was Jesus. His belief affected his vision, and he saw himself walking towards Jesus. His vision affected his attitude, as he replied, "Lord, tell me to come." His attitude affected his performance, as he got out of the boat. His performance affected his results, as he began to walk on the water. The same is true about his failure. His focus shifted away from his belief. This affected his vision, as he focused on the wind and waves. His vision affected his attitude, as he became afraid. His attitude affected his performance, as he began to sink. His performance affected his results, as he needed Jesus to save him.

Again, true belief drives action. Peter strongly believed it was indeed his Lord and that he could enable him to walk on water, and so he did. Peter also got distracted by the wind and waves and believed he couldn't, and so he did not. His belief greatly influenced his results. If you truly believe something, you will act according to that belief. Your actions are aligned with your true belief. Be careful what you allow into your belief system. Continue to believe and deepen your confidence in the aspects that will enable you to achieve your goals.

Beliefs can change. They can also grow and increase in strength. Your belief has the potential to destroy and remove doubt. Belief, faith, values, and principles are all siblings. They hang out on the playground of your mind, strengthening your ability to achieve your goals. Belief births confidence and grows into conviction. This confidence launches you forward into the next four principles that follow. Conviction is the strongest level of belief. It transports you to another dimension of belief because it does not compromise under any circumstance. Conviction caused Peter to step out of the boat and walk on the water in the midst of the storm. This was an excellent demonstration of conviction. It makes us realize beyond a shadow of a doubt that he believed in his Lord. If there were to be graduating class in the major of belief, conviction would receive the summa cum laude award, the highest honors.

Do you remember the story of the camel at the beginning of this chapter? The older traveler also demonstrated conviction. He had such strong belief in his advice that as a result he was able to convince the younger traveler to believe in his advice. His confidence was transferred to the young traveler, causing the young traveler to act on his advice. You need to have this kind of confidence and certainty, even when you don't have your rope, even when you don't see a way because life was designed to say "yes" to all of your dreams.

"A dream is created at least three times. First, it is fashioned in the mind. Next, it is designed on paper. Lastly, it is produced in reality."

CHAPTER TWO

Vision

(Belief, Vision, Attitude) + (Performance) = (Results)

Faith + Works = Success

The ability to see where you, your company, or organization can be tomorrow from where you are today can be extremely effective. It is the Creator giving you a glimpse of your future self today. It shows you a preview of what you are destined to become. It shows you the "I can" of the future. Your vision keeps you focused and keeps you attracted, pulling you in the direction of your goal. Vision breeds passion for what you do and serves as a motivator. It causes you to love what you do. Embracing vision along your journey can benefit you greatly. Vision helps you to keep fighting for your goals. Vision has many benefits. It allows you to keep your dream alive. It keeps you inspired.

There are many benefits of visions. It sharpens your perception. It improves how you see things. Vision allows you to see an opportunity where so many others may see an obstacle. Vision will act as the driving force behind your every action. Seeing the bigger picture in the back of your mind will get you through tough times. The bigger picture will be what keeps you going, keeps you fighting, and keeps you pushing for what you believe will eventually happen. If you believe something will happen, you will envision it. That vision enables you to be committed to your cause — to your goal. It enables you to see your goal through to the very end.

I like to say that a dream is created at least three times. First, it is created in the developer's mind. The developer sees it mentally. Then it is placed on paper or constructed as an architectural model — a mini physical representation of what is coming. After this, a contractor physically constructs it with the correct dimensions, size, etc. Vision gives life to your thoughts and ideas. It enables you to give birth to your dreams. For example, if you want to build a house, first you have the idea in your mind. Second, the architect draws up the blueprints for the home. Next, the contractor constructs the home. In some cases, another step may be made where an architectural model is presented. This principle can be compared to the pursuit of your own goals. It is first in your mind. Take it from your mind and place it onto paper. Your next step is to go and build your dream.

You may wonder, how can I keep my dream alive without any proof of the final product? There are a number of steps you can implement to hold your vision, such as the following:

- Create a vision board.
- Write down your vision.
- Incorporate it into your profile picture.
- Read your vision aloud every day.
- Integrate it into your workspace.
- Include it into your home space.

Create a vision board

A vision board is a representation of your hopes, dreams, and desires. It is usually a compilation of images, text, and photographs that represent what you want to achieve. There can be many aspects to your vision board. Some aspects of the goals represented on your vision board may be financial goals, family goals, travel goals, career goals, and parenting goals just to name a few. Without vision, you are likely to fail, and so a vision board holds that vision and reminds you of your goals. For many, vision boards are fun to create. It is a tool of motivation that reminds you of what you hope to achieve by the end of your journey. First, you must invest in a cork board or poster board. Second, create a compilation of text, images, and photos that represent your goals. Lastly, glue these to your poster board or cork board. Your board should help keep you in pursuit of your dreams.

Write down your vision

Writing down your goals on a daily basis can help you to visually see them. This can be extremely effective because seeing them will affect your subconscious in return, provoking you to be more productive. This method can also be effective in that it helps you to achieve the smaller goals leading up to the big ones. Create a checklist of your smaller goals. As you complete them, cross them off. This process encourages a clear and concise plan of action. It generates action steps that lead up to your final goal. Writing down your goals serves as a blueprint for getting the job done. Write down your goals leading up to the larger goals. Also, write down your final goals.

Incorporate it into your profile picture

Incorporating it into your social media's profile picture serves as a daily reminder. We use our social media accounts numerous times throughout the day. You're bound to be reminded of your vision if you incorporate it into the profile picture of your social media platforms. It may be a logo, an affirmation, or even a photo. Whatever representation you choose, ensure that it reminds you of why you started your pursuit. Ensure it reminds you to chase your dreams daily. It should provoke you to take consistent action every time you see it. This method propels you in the direction of your goals. It gives you stamina and keeps you determined towards your dreams.

Read your vision aloud daily

Reading your vision aloud can be highly effective in regard to your dreams. Stand in front of your mirror before you start your day and repeat your vision. "I'm going to pass my examinations." "I will land this job!" These are just examples and represent a powerful method that places you on the path to achievement. It affects your thought process by mentally reminding you of your purpose. Repeating your goals reminds you of your goals. This method reprograms the subconscious mind and prepares you to take action by motivating you, encouraging you, and boosting your self-esteem. Affirmations create a narrative for the individual. Within that narrative we see ourselves as capable of the desired achievement.

Integrate your vision in your work space

Integrating your vision into your work space gives you the right motivation at the ideal time. As you work, your vision is in sight at all times. Some ways you can do this are by having a framed photo, using a screen saver, or simply sticking it on the nearest wall. It can be your logo, business plan, a property you would like to purchase, etc. This keeps you going. It keeps you pushing. It keeps you motivated and in pursuit of your goal. Seeing your goal in your work space can trigger productive behavior and inspire action. It keeps your focus aligned and keeps you enthusiastic about your goals.

Include it into your home space

Including your vision into your home space gives you the right motivation the majority of the time. As you move about your home, your vision can be in sight at all times. Some ways you can do this are as follows:

- Keeping a framed photo or text in your bedroom, living area, dining area, etc.
- Incorporating it in items you may own, such as a mug with your logo.
- Displaying it on the fridge.

Seeing your goals in your home space reminds you and keeps you excited about your goals. This act can inspire daily action towards your goal.

Having a deep understanding of your end result is beyond vital to your journey. Vision helps you navigate your journey. Many may say that vision comes before belief. I accept that. However, the scrolls of wisdom tell us that we must walk by faith and not by sight. Faith is different from logic. Logic says, "I will only do this if this makes sense." Faith says, "I believe this will happen no matter what," and "I will fight for this no matter the circumstances I face."

Vision keeps you focused and motivated. Because vision serves as a source of inspiration, it keeps you going. Just as future home owners can gain inspiration from the architectural drawings of their future homes, you too can gain inspiration from the vision you hold regarding your goal. Think of the details and dynamics of your goal. Think of the specifics and particulars that get you excited when you ponder the ultimate outcome. Your vision is the manifestation of an already completed journey. It urges you forward because it reminds you of what is coming. The sense of empowerment that vision brings with it pushes you forward, causing you to become deeply engaged in the possibility of birthing your goal.

Sometimes it may be hard to hold that mental snapshot of your goal, but press on and allow the power of belief to fuel your vision. Allow yourself moments to reflect on the dream within you. Every step you take toward your goal will be as a result of the vision you hold. Your vision gives you meaning. Vision unlocks the inspiration you need to keep going so that no matter what you are going through, you have the tools you need to mentally keep pushing forward. See yourself holding that Olympic medal. See yourself as that medical doctor. See yourself behind the desk of that job position you desire. See yourself as the head of your very own company. You should see your dream so clearly that your actions become a deliberate and specific move that pushes you in the direction of achievement. Become obsessed with your vision. Become infatuated with seeing yourself at the end of the finish line. Realize that your current situation is not permanent but temporary. Master the art of seeing beyond. This skill of second sight carries you through. This is what you were born to do. This is your purpose. God gave you this. Embrace it. Accept it. Fight for it. Envision it clearly every day so it becomes a part of you.

Vision is so powerful that it can carry you throughout your journey. A vision is the utilization of a mental picture of a condition that is desired. Your vision serves as a compass that guides you in the direction of this goal. It is like a miniature painting of the bigger picture that you keep in the back of your mind while you work to put together the physical pieces of the puzzle, so that eventually the bigger picture can be achieved in the physical realm. The more you reach into the back of your mind and retrieve this bigger picture, the more you feel inspired and motivated to press on toward your goal. And when you feel like quitting, that mental picture comes into focus once again leading you to act, to continue in pursuit of your aspiration. The principle of vision guides you in the direction of the task you must complete.

During my time at the Eight-Mile Rock High School, the District Educational Officer visited and spoke to us on the topic of "Greatness." At the end of his speech, he asked each child, "What do you want to be when you grow up?"

Now, I was known to be a class clown and wanted to live up to that standard. I replied, "I would like to be a professional bum. I would like to beg people for money."

He looked at me and said, "Oh, you want to deal with money!" He continued, "I can see you one day working as a professional in the arena of banking and finance."

Today, I have made a pretty successful career in the field of collections. What does a collector do? A collector professionally asks people for money.

The speaker who spoke to us repeatedly told us, "I see something in you." This was a reminder of the greatness that was planted within us. This reminder gave us hope. We looked forward to embracing the greatness they spoke of. My response of wanting to be a professional bum was a smart-mouthed one; however, the speaker was able to see beyond my antics and generated a vision that was destined to become my reality. He was able to see a respectable objective beyond my playfulness.

Take a closer look at the glass half full/glass half empty theory. The optimist may view the glass as half full because the optimist tends to be confident about the future. The pessimist may view the glass as half empty because the pessimist tends to believe the worst will happen. I take the view of the dreamer because the dreamer tends to have a purpose-driven point of view. The dreamer asks, what are you trying to accomplish? What is your aim? What is really going on with the glass of water? An experiment may be taking place in order to determine how much rain can fill the glass within a specific time frame. An experiment may also be taking place in order to determine how much water will evaporate after leaving the glass in the sun within a specific time frame. The dreamer determines which half is open to interpretation. The dreamer asks, "What is the aim behind this?" The dreamer wants to determine whether your objective is to get the glass full or empty. The dreamer then aligns your aim with the objective. The glass may have been sitting there under the open skies as an experiment in order to determine how long it would take to fill the glass or how long it would take to measure the evaporation process.

Once the dreamer understands this, he would then place his focus on the objective and purpose and realize you have arrived at your halfway mark. The dreamer realizes that you are halfway to your goal no matter which experiment is taking place. Embrace how far you have come and not how far you are behind. Always see the progress you are making towards your goal. Don't be quick to judge and not see opportunity. How you see life is going to affect how you approach life When you see situations, try to understand the aim. Try to understand what is going on. Realize the objective and then act accordingly.

Vision can take the smallest and seemingly insignificant idea and elevate it, making it absolutely special. Have a vision for yourself, but also understand that there are times when others can also see the potential in you. This is something that should be embraced and should be practiced in our view of others as well. Call out the greatness you see in others in order to help get them there. Encourage them to stay the course. Spot it in others and help them to recognize their own potential in the same way the District Education Officer spotted it in me. When we do this, we increase the probability of another's success.

"Are you prepared to do what it takes for as long as it takes until you achieve your goal?"

CHAPTER THREE

Attitude

(Belief, Vision, Attitude) + (Performance) = (Results)

Faith + Works = Success

The tale is told of young Johnny, who decided that he would attend the school dance. Now, Johnny was not very popular; however, he loved to dance. When he got to the dance, Johnny took to the dance floor and unleashed his best moves. After quite some time, he realized that it takes two to tango. It was no fun dancing alone, and Johnny wanted a dancing partner. He danced toward Susan, carefully placing one foot in front of the other in perfect timing with the music.

Susan giggled as he gracefully extended his hand toward her. She politely shook her head and declined his offer.

Johnny danced his way back to the middle of the dance floor. His feelings were bruised, but he continued to rock back and forth to the upbeat music. He swayed left and then right as he worked up the courage to ask another young lady to dance with him. Slowly, he danced toward Deloris. Johnny dipped low and bounced in Deloris' direction. Gently taking her hand, he started to pull her towards the dance floor.

Deloris yanked her hand away before walking away in disgust.

Johnny slowly rocked back and forth in shock. Ignoring the laughter that arose in the room, he began to dance stronger than ever before. The crowd began to cheer as he unleashed more of his finest moves. Johnny noticed Cynthia dancing across the floor. He danced towards Cynthia. He dipped. He began to spin, then dipped again. Lower this time. "Great moves," he shouted above the music, then asked, "Would you like to dance?"

Cynthia smiled shyly before accepting his extended arm.

Everyone cheered. Johnny finally had a dancing partner!

What was Johnny's goal? "I would like a dancing partner." Why did Johnny succeed? Because he held the belief that at least one of the young ladies would dance with him. What kept Johnny going? Because he held the vision, "I see myself dancing with at least one of these beautiful young ladies." What was his attitude? "I am prepared to ask each of them until one of them says yes." What did this lead to? "I will give it my best every time." What was the result of this? Johnny had a dancing partner before the night ended. This example is a lot like life. No matter how unattainable our goals may seem I encourage you to adopt Johnny's attitude of sticking with it until he got it. Although this example is just a simple dance, the principle of pressing forward despite rejection is a powerful one and can be applied to life. Train yourself to not give up until you receive the "yes" that life has to offer no matter how challenging your goal may seem. Believe in your goal. See your capacity to achieve that goal. Keep pressing on, and your victory will come.

Your attitude is the most influential aspect of your journey. You may want the success and achievement attached to a goal, but ask yourself whether you are prepared to do what it takes for as long as it takes until you achieve your goal. Imagine if Johnny had decided he would take the shy approach rather than the attitude of boldness. Imagine if he had cowered in the corner and whispered his request rather than boldly asking each girl to dance. Over the course of your journey, you will discover that having the correct attitude will greatly impact the momentum of your voyage. Attitude speaks to your commitment and your approach just as Johnny displayed. Not only to your goal but also to each challenge that may arise before its achievement. Most goals consist of tiny steps that lead to one big picture. For example, a medical student must pass a number of theoretical and practical examinations before gaining a medical degree. All examinations require students to release their best study habits until the task of passing that examination is completed. Sound familiar? How about when an entrepreneur's goal is to land a client? Pitching, marketing, networking, and promotion must be successful before a client is on boarded. Landing a client is the big goal. The tiny steps such as pitching, marketing, networking, and promotion lead up to the bigger goal of landing the client. Are you pitching with the perfect strategy? Are you putting one hundred percent into your marketing campaigns? Are you networking all the time? Are you using promotion tools that are effective? Are you giving out business cards? Are you sharing your website's link? Are you handing out brochures that detail your products and services? What is your attitude towards the tiny steps? What is your approach in the smaller tasks that lead up to the final achievement?

Attitude is a mental posture or stance that affects the way you advance toward a situation. It affects the way you approach each challenge you encounter on your journey. Along the way, you will discover just how vital attitude is and how fundamentally crucial having the correct attitude is to your goal. Attitude influences behavior. Say to yourself, "I will do whatever it takes for as long as it takes until I achieve my goal." Your attitude is a good predictor of the behavior you will display toward your goal. It structures your journey and provokes action that propels you forward toward your dreams.

There is a story that tells us of two neighbors Bob and Elizabeth. One evening after midnight, Elizabeth's mom flew into town for a surprise visit. Elizabeth realized that she did not have sufficient food to offer her mom. Also, much to her dismay, the stores were closed. Elizabeth decided to pay Bob a visit since Bob was a baker and baked regularly. She knocked desperately on his door. A red-eyed, sleepy Bob answered. After apologizing for disturbing him so late, Elizabeth calmly asked Bob if he could spare a loaf of bread.

"I'm sleeping!" Bob replied groggily. He shut the door, leaving a helpless Elizabeth on the door step to figure out her next move.

Elizabeth knocked again. There was no answer. After about three knocks, she knocked more rapidly.

Bob yanked open the door angrily. "I'm trying to sleep!" he nearly shouted and slammed the door.

As Elizabeth left Bob's yard, she felt helpless. However, she decided to try Mary who lived across the street. "Mary!" she called. There was no answer. Elizabeth knocked loudly. She noticed Mary's lights were on; however there simply was no answer. Loud music echoed through the house drowning out Elizabeth's calls. She desperately looked up and down the street. "I know," she thought to herself. "I'll try Mrs. Bain." Elizabeth ran frantically towards Mrs. Bain's home. "Mrs. Bain!" she called out. She knocked loudly. Mrs. Bain answered sleepily. Elizabeth calmly explained her situation and then made her request. "Can you please spare a bite to eat for my mother?" She waited quietly.

"Sure," Mrs. Bain replied.

Elizabeth sighed happily as Mrs. Bain filled a large grocery bag with a loaf of bread, a slab of cheese, and a large portion of ham. She even threw in a carton of orange juice. Elizabeth was ecstatic. "We'll make ham and cheese sandwiches!" she said excitedly. She thanked Mrs. Bain and returned to her mother.

The moral of this story is that persistence is key to success. Like Johnny, Elizabeth was prepared to do what it took for as long as it took until she got what she wanted. She did not allow Bob's rudeness to discourage her. She didn't allow the late midnight hour to stop her from approaching Mrs. Bain and making her request. Just as Elizabeth and Johnny received their yes, the yes of life is there for you as well. Believe it and be determined to achieve it despite the obstacles that will come. Don't let discouragement destroy you. Discouragement is real, but don't let it paralyze you. Do not let it cause you to stop. Many have terminated their destiny by allowing discouragement to stop them. Nothing in life is as strong as a mind made up. Be persistent in chasing your goals. Do not let discouragement cause you to quit. Like Elizabeth and Johnny, you will eventually succeed.

Life recognizes persistence. Persistence assists you in achieving your goals. You may have to go through hundreds of rejections until you get your "yes." Remember your "yes" is out there, you just have to find it. Keep pushing. Keep pressing. Don't give up. Be persistent. Keep knocking on the door of success. Many individuals give up and leave too soon. Many stop knocking and give up too quickly.

Success can often be compared to an elderly person. Imagine going to the home of an elderly person and knocking on their door. They hear you, but they have to make preparations to receive you. Success is like an elderly person coming to answer the door. Before coming to the door, the elderly need to find their glasses.

They have to put on their bath robe. They have to put in their dentures. They need to find their bedroom slippers. They have to find their walking cane. They must do all of these things before they slowly shuffle to the door. They may even be calling out, "I'm coming!" As the voice of an elderly person is low, you may not hear them; however, they are preparing themselves to answer you.

Life is the same way. Life is slow. It is preparing itself to answer you, and just because you don't see or hear anything happening doesn't mean there is no progress. Life slowly prepares itself to answer you. If you're patient, you may sometimes see a small sign that they are coming. If you wait patiently and take a closer look, you may see a light turn on. You may ask, what is a more practical example of a sign? Here is one. A college student may have completed two years out of a four-year degree and is on the verge of giving up. Should they give up? No. A sign that the degree is coming is that two years of the time has already been successfully completed. If the student patiently waits and continues to be dedicated to the task, then he or she will eventually receive the reward they desire.

The same concept applies when the elderly prepares to answer the door. They are deliberate and intentional in their actions, but they will get there to answer you. You will not be able to see or hear all that is happening behind the door. Sometimes by the time an elderly person gets to the door, we are gone. Life is the same way. Sometimes we give up too soon. Trust the process. Everything is coming together for your success. Life is preparing to answer you. It is slowly preparing itself to open the door you have been knocking on. Don't give up too soon. Success, like the elderly, may take long to come to the door, but eventually success will get there to answer you. Don't stop knocking too soon. Do whatever it takes for as long as it takes until you have achieved your goal.

The brain needs to be mentally strengthened to endure the journey of finding the "yes" life has to offer. Here is an example of how you can train your mind to always look for the "yes." Your mind is like a computer. If you type the letter "A" into the Google Search, guess what comes up? You will see lots of words beginning with the letter "A." Page one may have words and phrases that include the letter "A." From "auto" to "airlines" you will see lots of "A" words. Page 9 will also give you "A" words such as "apply" and "ads." Why do you think this is? This is because you searched for the letter "A." The search engine is designed to deliver exactly what you requested from it. The search is programmed to deliver what you tell it to. The mind works the same way. You would agree that the reason only words beginning with the letter "A" came up is because Google searched all possibilities and scenarios of what you typed in.

Let's use a more practical example. Let's say you're on vacation and you are considering participating in an activity that terrifies you. If you're like me, an activity like sailing. If you are terrified, your mind will search for all the possibilities as to why you should not go sailing. If you tell yourself you cannot go sailing, your brain will come up with all kinds of reasons for you not to sail. "It is hurricane season" may be one reason. "It's not safe" may be another reason. You may also consider the possibility of getting lost at sea or even being accidentally thrown overboard. The reverse is also true if you tell yourself that you can go sailing. Your mind will come up with all kinds of reasons as to why you should sail. "You can sail when hurricane season is over" may be one reason. Another reason might be "You can be safe by utilizing life vests, life boats, etc." Your mind may also think of utilizing a GPS system to help you navigate your sailing trip. Also, you can ensure that your sailboat is fully equipped with a lifebuoy and other sailing essentials.

Your brain is programmed to deliver exactly what you tell it to. Having a yes attitude helps you to realize that for every "cannot" there is a "can." See the "cannot" and the "can" as two sides of the same coin. One side of the coin reflects that you cannot, and the flip side of the coin reflects that you can. Because the yes and no attitude are two sides of the same coin, then if you can see the no/can't, you also have the ability to see the yes/can. It is the yes attitude that helps you to find the solutions to the challenges you will face. There is always a solution to your fears. I encourage you to be solution oriented during your journey to success. Whether you tell yourself that something can happen or cannot happen, your mind will come up with a million reasons why. Tell yourself why you can rather than why you can't. Do not shut down your victory before you even give it a chance. Don't jump to the conclusion that it is impossible. Do not allow tough tasks and weighted goals to discourage you. Train yourself to always look for the possibility. Train yourself to always seek the "yes."

There are times when you will need to fine tune, tweak, strengthen, and maybe even revise your strategy in order to achieve success. Remember the story of Johnny? Johnny learned a valuable lesson after each rejection. He strengthened his approach. First, he extended his hand to the young lady and was rejected. On the second try, he gently took the young lady's hand only to be rejected again. On the third try, he showcased his moves, complimented his desired, and asked the young lady if she would like to dance before extending his arm. Take note that his goal was to get a dance; however, in this case he had to tweak his strategy to achieve his goal. His dream did not change, but every time he failed he improved on his next attempt. His success was tied to fine tuning and perfecting his approach. Each time he tried again, he executed his approach with more confidence and a more strategic and dynamic appeal. The same can be applied to your own journey. Your goal may not change, but in the event of failure and rejection you have to be able to adapt in order to achieve your success. Like the popular saying goes "There is more than one way to skin a cat." Adapting can be anything that increases your probability of accomplishment. It may be returning to college and getting that degree you need. It can be attending that live training or hiring a personal coach. It could be earning that license in order to sell your products and services on a wider scale. Whatever it is, do it so that you are able to achieve your desired success. Do the necessary in order to excel in the next level of your journey.

There will be many challenges but, having a positive attitude is key. Let us take a look at how having a positive attitude helped my childhood and early career mentor Leon Williams pilot the treacherous storms life can bring.

"At every twist and turn, life throws curve balls and adversities at you. I lost jobs, my dear Son, Mother, and Father (my mentor). My positive attitude, fueled by my faith, has been a big part of the DNA of my success and leadership style and has allowed me to successfully navigate many challenges."

Leon R. Williams

Former CEO (Two-Time) Bahamas Telecommunications Company Ltd. (BTC) & SVP Cable & Wireless Communications Plc

Former Chairman (Two-Time) Caribbean Association of National Telecommunication Organizations (CANTO)

Person of the Year Bahamas 2014

Having a good attitude is important and will get you through tough times. During these tough times you may want to give up but, remain anchored in the belief that it is possible and grounded in the likelihood of your vision.

"Hard work may go unrewarded for awhile, but it will not go unrewarded forever."

CHAPTER FOUR

Performance

(Belief, Vision, Attitude) + (Performance) = (Results)

Faith + Works = Success

Performance speaks to giving it your best all day every day. Choose to deliver at a level that exceeds expectations every time. The scrolls of wisdom tell us that faith without works is dead. A great performance is key to achieving your goal because this is where success lies. Results and success can be used interchangeably. Unlike the first three principles in the *Maximum Me* formula that exemplify mindset, performance epitomizes action. It is the driving force that brings home results. A consistent and dynamic performance will usually bring about excellent results.

Never stop trying to improve your performance. How well you execute your task is aligned with the results you will achieve. Give it one hundred percent every time. Give it your absolute best every single day. Sharpen your skills. Do this consistently, and your results will be nothing short of astounding. Have confidence in knowing that you will succeed because success comes in small steps. Confidence says, "If I am successful at this level then there is a good chance that I can be successful when pursuing the next level." Performance also speaks to growth and achievement. For this part of your journey, your goal depends heavily on the application of all of your knowledge and the execution of skills when completing each task leading up to the achievement of your goal. Performance is the delivery method that takes action and uses it to gain growth and achievement. When we meet the standard of excellence, growth and achievement is possible. Life presents many challenges; however, a champion performance can consistently overcome most trials. An incredibly intricate performance trumps most challenges. Be committed to your course of action. The distance your dream goes depends on the effort you put behind it. Perspiration, determination, and grit are needed to help your dream take flight.

An old story tells us of an excellent and skilled contractor who worked for the owner of one of the top construction companies for many years. His work exceeded all expectations, and he was highly paid. The owner of the company was retiring, and he wanted to do something special for the contractor before he retired. He thought about it for a while. After some time, he asked the contractor to build one last house. "Build it as if you are building your dream home," he said to him. "Spare no expense."

Now, the contractor thought to himself, "I am his longest serving employee, and my work has made him very rich. He is retiring, but he gave no assurance as to whether my future is secured." The contractor became angry and spiteful when he thought of this. He sought to take his revenge. He built the house but took it upon himself to produce poor quality work. When building the home, he decided to cut corners and reduce the quality of his work because of his frustration.

Upon completion of the home, the owner came, got the keys and inspected the house. Although he was not pleased with the workmanship, he did not express his disappointment. In fact, he called the contractor and asked, "Are you happy with the final product?"

Now the contractor knew that he had not done superb quality work, but he replied and said, "I am extremely pleased with this home."

The owner then gave him the keys and said, "This home is my present to you for your many years of faithful service. The home, my friend, is yours."

The contractor was flabbergasted. He regretted his actions drastically.

Sometimes we may think we are not being fully rewarded; however, in spite of this, we should continue to do well and give it our best every time. There are times when you cannot see your reward right away. Even though you cannot see your reward, you should continue to do your best. You never know when your reward is about to come. In addition, you must remember at all times that your reputation is on the line. Your work is a representation of you. As long as you're going to do something, do it to the best of your ability. I acknowledge that it is hard, but it is the right thing to do. You are building your character, your integrity, and your standard when you agree to execute a task. It is better to not agree to do the task than to show up and not give your best. It is also better to quit the job than to start the job and not complete it to the best of your ability. The quality of your work is your signature. This is what others will know you by. Give good quality work every time. Yes, you are certain to have some bad days. But, don't allow a circumstance to change your attitude to one of giving a poor standard of work. It is better for you to leave that company than to stay and do a mediocre job.

Giving good quality work can be the reason why another company may seek you out. They don't seek you out because you work for a great company, they seek you out because they believe you helped that company to become great. All great companies have three things in common:

- They have a great vision.
- They have great challenges.
- They have great employees to execute that vision and overcome those challenges.

Successful companies need employees who are dedicated to giving an excellent performance. Most prosperous enterprises are a result of an excellent performance given by a unified team devoted to performing each given task to the best of their ability. I encourage you to use every ounce of effort when accomplishing each task presented to you. Giving every ounce of effort every single time enables you to never miss a single opportunity that may lie in your favor. The contractor's story is the perfect example of this. If a potential client asks the contractor to show the last home he built, the results would more than likely be devastating. He is almost guaranteed not to get the job. It would have been better for the contractor to not have built that house. His integrity and his career-long reputation of being a top quality contractor could now be at risk because he did not give that one job his best.

Before you get so discouraged to the point where you allow your performance to deteriorate far below your standard on a consistent basis, it is better for you to leave. Don't allow a circumstance to change your attitude because your attitude affects your performance. You may not always see the opportunity at first. Some opportunities hide behind a job well done. Some rewards are given after a job is completed in excellence. Galatians 6:9 tells us, "To not become weary in doing good, for at the proper time we will reap a harvest if we do not give up." Do not become frustrated and tired if you do not receive your reward right away. Keep working, your reward is coming. An opportunity may present itself at any time. Giving one hundred percent effort every single time enables you to be ready the moment it arrives. This persistent effort helps to equip you with the dynamic portfolio you will need when an opportunity seeks you out. This effort may also determine how big your reward will be.

I am reminded of a popular story of a young bank teller named Anne. Anne was a great teller; however, Anne was wishy-washy when it came to customer service. Some days, Anne smiled and gave one hundred percent. Other days, Anne felt as though her pay was not worth the stress some customers put her through. On Mondays, Tuesdays, and Wednesdays, Anne was annoyed mainly because it was the beginning of the week. However, she absolutely loved Thursdays and Fridays. She giggled and smiled on the days closer to the end of the week. On these day, she got tons of quality referrals for loans, mortgages, credit cards, and deposit accounts. Anne practiced this bi-polar service regularly, and in due time it became a part of who she was as an employee. In the span of the two days, she did put her best foot forward she met her target goals, so her numbers were still high. But despite her high numbers, Anne was not chosen on three separate occasions for the promotion she wanted.

One Monday morning, Anne stood at her wicket frowning. She considered Monday to be the worst day of the week. "Next in line," she called. She sorted through her past customer receipts as she waited for the next person in line to come. Nothing. "Next in line!" Anne called louder this time.

"Good morning!" exclaimed a middle-aged gentleman as he approached her teller wicket.

"How can I help you?" Anne replied dryly.

"Ah yes, I would like to change one thousand dollars into

smaller notes please."

Anne studied the requested breakdown of the cash. The customer wanted two bundles of twenty-five cents, two-and-a-half bundles of ten cents, five bundles of five cents, and six hundred dollars in singles. Anne rolled her eyes because she would have to go to the cashiers' cage in order to fulfill her customer's order. She laughed and chatted with the cage teller even after receiving the cash. Twenty-five minutes went by. "He should have expected a long wait," she told herself as she returned glumly to her wicket.

"I would also like to make a withdrawal of three thousand dollars," Anne's customer said as he removed his debit card from his wallet.

Anne sighed heavily. The moment he swiped his card, Anne noticed the enormous amount on his account. Five million dollars was in the deposit account. His profile read Mr. Jack Smith, C.E.O of Jack & Smith Security Firms. Anne's supervisor walked by at that very moment.

"Good morning, Mr. Smith!" she called cheerily. "What brings you to us today?"

"Oh, a little mystery shopping," he replied. Anne's heart sank. "I'm looking for a new executive assistant," he continued.

"That's amazing," Anne's supervisor replied. "How was your service today?"

Mr. Smith looked at Anne. "It was okay," he said before walking away.

Anne's supervisor whispered, "Watch out for that one. He took our last girl by offering her double pay!"

Anne blinked in disbelief as she realized her poor performance may have cost her the job of a lifetime.

Notice that Anne had the potential of giving excellent customer service, but her performance was inconsistent. The day she let her guard down was the day she missed her opportunity.

Give a good performance consistently, not only because your present employer is watching you, but because your potential employer may be watching you also. Opportunities seek you out when you give it your best all the time. Make it a habit to produce good work. Strive to execute beyond the level of your pay grade every day. Executing beyond your pay grade enables you to stand out as an expert in your industry. It allows others to notice you. You command attention when you give a superstar performance. Let your value outweigh your pay. Be faithful to giving a good performance, no matter the circumstances. This may seem unrealistic, but in the end it is absolutely worth it. When you are paid more than you are worth, you make an excellent candidate for termination, especially in tough times. When you are paid as much as you are worth, you get stagnated. When you outweigh your pay, what you bring to the table becomes highly valuable. Operating beyond your pay grade isn't a bad thing. Hard work may go unrewarded for a while, but it will not go unrewarded forever.

Work hard and work well, even if:

- You are not rewarded fairly.
- You feel unappreciated.
- You are overlooked for a promotion.

Give it your best no matter what because sooner or later one of the following will happen:

- Someone else will recognize your talent.

- Bosses will eventually recognize your value.
- Your boss may be replaced.

There are times when those in higher positions than us keep these rewards from us. However, eventually these rewards do indeed arrive at their destination. Continue to perform well despite how you are treated. If you get frustrated and begin to perform poorly, there will be just cause to terminate you. The moment you limit your performance, you do a greater injustice to yourself than someone else can ever do to you. Popular advice may tell you, “Don’t perform beyond expectations. Be exact and perform according to your pay grade.” The best form of job security is an excellent performance. Work to the best of your ability consistently. As an individual who hopes to be promoted to the next level in the workplace or in entrepreneurship, you have the ability to do three things.

- Learn a task: Growth
- Master that task: Value
- Teach/Train someone else to do that task: Legacy

Learn a Task: Growth

Acquiring a skill that utilizes your potential adds to your value and enables your growth. Developing a skill set can help you in many ways. It signifies your willingness to execute a talent that provides value to your clients and organization, whether you are an entrepreneur or an employee. Your skill set provides value to your clients. When you gain a skill, you gain an advantage.

Self-development makes you more valuable. It enhances you. The act of learning a task places you in a position of progression. Be committed to dominating your territory in all aspects so that true growth can be accelerated. This is key to your voyage because it makes you more adaptable, giving you the means to be more flexible in your position. New tasks and skills increase your portfolio's credibility, diversity, and appeal. Learn as many tasks as you can. Ensure that they are essential to your journey. This in and of itself gives you a learning experience that is unique and dynamic.

Don't be fearful of making mistakes when you are learning a task. Truth be told, you will make some mistakes. Like I often say, "Failure taken in the right perspective often brings success." Mistakes are a part of the learning process. This is how you grow and develop. In addition, don't be overly anxious to have achieved the speed your peers may have. Speed will become an asset, but it is more important to learn the task correctly. When you are learning a task, your priority should be accuracy and then speed. Eventually you will possess both accuracy and speed. The moment this happens is the moment you know you are on your way to mastering that task.

Master that Task: Value

Becoming undeniably efficient plays a role when paving the way for your success. When people think of your industry, do they think of you, or do they think of someone else? You may not be the best, but be at your best. Mastering the skills you have obtained gives rise to your worth. A part of the mastering process also lies in mastering your attitude and conduct. Doing so assists you in commanding the respect you deserve. The value you bring is determined by how well you master your skill set and conduct.

When you are able to contribute efficiently to your industry, you become invaluable. If you are efficient and effective in your arena, then progression to the next level most likely will follow.

Being able to complete and execute each task efficiently is a good indicator that you have potential for the next level. Demonstrate confidence when performing each task you take on. Execute with exceptional competency, incomparable capability, and unrivaled proficiency. This makes you priceless. This ensures you are fully compensated for your contribution almost every time. Also, don't be discouraged if you are overlooked. I know that being overlooked can be frustrating. It can be infuriating when a boss, coach, or higher authority does not give you the credit you deserve. Attempt to do your best in spite of this. Strive to become even better despite this. Someone else will eventually recognize your value and pay you well for the results you are capable of bringing to the table. The territory of achievement goes beyond the dimension of the organization you work for. There is a territory outside your department. There is a territory outside your organization. And there is a territory outside your country.

I once heard a popular celebrity say, "Hard work beats talent when talent doesn't work hard." This simply means not to worry if another individual is more gifted or talented than you. Yes, they may be more gifted than you, but if you always bring your best and one day they don't bring their best, then that is the day you outperform that individual. Bring your best every day because life is similar to a decathlon. A decathlon is a combined event consisting of ten track and field events. During this event, performance is judged according to a points system. It is not judged according to the participant's achieved position. Therefore, winners are determined by the combined performance in all events. You don't have to be the best in all ten events to become the champion of the decathlon. You just have to do well in all of them. Do your best in everything you do.

Train/Teach Someone Else: Legacy

This next step is the last piece of the puzzle regarding the cycle of growth and development. This is your legacy — a way for you to propel the next generation forward. It is fulfilling to know that you have helped someone. Train others so that you can be replaced by them whether through promotion or retirement. Prepare your replacement to perform the tasks with excellence in the same way you do. Most individuals who fail to pass on their knowledge and expertise refuse to do so because:

- They are fearful that they will lose their job. (If you can train one, you can train one hundred, and you become more valuable to that organization. Change your mindset and lose the fear. As an executive I can almost guarantee you that you will not lose your job for adapting the principle of training someone else.)
- They believe that they are more valuable to that organization if they are the only one who can complete that task. (This is a huge myth. While in the short term they may seem invaluable, sooner or later the organization will realize that you are not a developer of people and won't propel you forward. The higher you go, the more you will need to provide more training, coaching, guidance, and mentoring to others. You will not excel and your team will not consistently perform at the highest level if you are unable to apply this principle.)

Passing on your knowledge and skills guarantees a replacement when you are moved to the next level. What makes this so momentous? It makes your organization less vulnerable when you have a trained replacement who is ready and able to fully execute at your level. This guaranteed replacement in return guarantees your progression, fast-tracking it in a way you probably never imagined. Your training abilities are valuable. If you are mastering your task, and you train twelve people to master that same task, then you have created twelve leaders who can lead in that area.

There is a story about a junior accountant by the name of John. John worked for one of the top major accounting firms in the country. John was an excellent employee and had long mastered the skills and knowledge of his expertise. He was well versed in financial reporting, had strong problem-solving and analytical skills, and his ability to work under pressure was immaculate. John, however, refused to train anyone to do his job. He felt threatened by the idea of another person being just as efficient as he was. In addition, he had applied many times for a senior accountant position to no avail. His last performance appraisal report had excellent results, and so this left John confused. He knew he was more than capable of succeeding in this position, but he did not receive the promotion. This bothered John so much that one day he gathered his courage to ask his supervisor why he was overlooked for the position he felt he rightfully deserved.

His supervisor got two chairs and placed them side by side. He began to explain. "The red chair represents your current position as junior accountant. The blue chair represents the desired position of senior accountant. The red chair makes me two dollars. The blue chair makes me three dollars. Together both chairs make me five dollars. If I move you to the blue chair, who then will fill your position in the red chair?"

John was silent for a moment. "Sally," he replied.

His supervisor shook his head. "Sally isn't fully trained," he replied. "We have invested and fully trained you. However, you have not invested and trained Sally. Sally will only make me one dollar." He paused as John thought about what he had said. "If I move Sally while she is untrained, then both chairs together will make me four dollars. If I do this, I will lose money."

John thought about it for some time.

"Do you understand?" his supervisor asked. "It is a business decision. Train Sally to perform exceptionally well. Teach her how to exceed expectations when meeting targets. Equip her so that she is able to make me two dollars the moment I place her into your chair," he said. "In fact, if you train Sally and Sue to make me two dollars in the red chair, you would have proven yourself beyond valuable to the regard of both performance and training. Also, when you are ready to move even beyond the blue chair, Sally's chair will still be covered the moment she is ready to progress to the red chair."

It was then that John finally understood the importance of training a replacement— his progression depended on it. He realized that in addition to giving a good performance, it is also important to train others. He then made up his mind to train Sally and Sue to execute his job to the best of their abilities.

These three action steps embody a cycle within itself — a cycle of growth. This cycle represents an evolution of development and advancement. Learning a task, mastering that task, then training someone else to do that task are three action steps that can almost every time transport you to the next level. It is important that you are learning for your next position, mastering the position you are in, and teaching others so that you can be replaced (not in the aspect of being terminated, but in the aspect of being promoted). I can assure you that in all of my years of business, I have rarely seen a person let go as a result of good performance.

Your ability to train is valuable. This is a capacity that affords the company you work for the opportunity to be top in its industry.

So, lose the fear of termination and operate to the best of your ability to learn a task, master that task, and teach someone else. It is when these three steps are satisfied, opportunity seeks you out and enables you to progress. Understand that these steps are crucial to the progress and further development of an individual. It is when you have done these three action steps that you are truly ready to be promoted to the next level.

You may be a poor performer today, but you still have the potential to be a star performer tomorrow. Also, you may be a star performer today and give a poor performance tomorrow. Know that things can turn around even if you have a history of poor performance. Believe it, begin to see it, and your attitude will change. This will help your performance to turn around. Your previous performance does not necessarily guarantee continued performance. Allow me to share a few of my accomplishments for the purpose of emphasizing this point. Even though I am an accomplished banker, there was a time when I struggled badly, and it appeared I would not make it.

Some years ago, I was given the opportunity to become branch manager of one of the bank's branches. I was happy for the opportunity although the branch presented many challenges. At the end of the year, the audit report was not a good one. I had failed as a leader. My branch had not given a good performance. I was called into the office of the then district manager and was accompanied by my supervisor at the time. As I sat in the meeting, I grumbled and created excuses. I also pointed out all of the challenges and obstacles that I had inherited when I took over the branch. I also blamed everyone from my superiors to my staff and offered no possible solution.

The district manager shook his head. "I am even more concerned now than when I first read this poor audit report," he said.

The district manager was awed by my attitude and poor approach to my poor results. He became even more concerned because I was not taking responsibility for anything.

My supervisor gathered that the district manager was frustrated and recognized his point. She then realized that at that moment I could have possibly talked myself into getting fired. She requested a break from the meeting and gave me some of the greatest advice I have ever encountered in my career. She took me back into her office, and for the next hour or so she coached me through my circumstance.

"The reason I stopped the meeting is because it was not going well. You weren't taking any responsibility for the poor audit report. You focused on what is going wrong. The bad report is yesterday, but if we have the right mindset we can change our performance and change the results." She presented each challenge the branch had faced and asked "What would you do to fix this?"

As we spoke, my mindset changed and my confidence in my ability was renewed. I was now able to find a reasonable and practical solution to each challenge. I had a solution for every problem she mentioned.

She called the district manager and requested to resume the meeting. It was then I was able to continue with a solution-oriented mindset. My approach changed. I apologized for the bad report and presented an action plan as to how I would turn the poor audit around.

The district manager's face once again was in awe; however, this time it was due to amazement. He was pleased to see that we now had a game plan that would work. He recognized my transformed attitude and dedication to changing my performance and commended me for it.

Shortly after this experience, my performance began to improve, and eventually my team and I were able to make a complete and impressive turnaround. The following year we received a nomination for the "Branch of the Year" award, and through consistent performance we have gone on to win the award an unprecedented number of times. Through coaching, perseverance and persistent performance, my team and I produced the best turnaround results that year and later went on to win the "Branch of the Year" award more times than any other team during my tenure as branch manager. I want to encourage you to embody the mindset of "How can I fix this?" when you are faced with similar obstacles. In my experience, I had failed; however, I was able to turn that failure into success by changing my attitude and my performance.

Failure

Don't be afraid of failure. Failure can be an excellent teacher. As I mentioned before, "When viewed in the right perspective, failure often brings success." When you fail at a task, try again. Keep trying until you are successful at attaining your goal. Keep going. There is a universe of possibilities. Learn from your failure. Use it to educate and shape your next attempt. Use it to clarify your goal, eliminate the error, and improve your methods. A mistake can be viewed as an error, or it can be viewed as a valuable lesson that you can apply to your next shot. Failure deepens your knowledge regarding the journey you are taking. It often reveals to you the correct way, points out something you didn't know, and shows you something you missed. Using failure to shape your future attempts can give you new insight and awareness that you may not have had before. The process of failure is designed to make you more knowledgeable. It is designed to teach and educate you regarding your goal. Repurpose your failure. Determine why your faulty methods did not work. Use this knowledge to find the correct solution to achieving your goal. Failure strengthens your problem-solving skills, analytical skills, and provokes your determination to find a solution. It gives you the wisdom you need to move forward. Failure gives you a clear understanding of how you should proceed.

There is a difference between failing and failed. You may be failing now, but it is not until you quit that you have failed. You may not be doing well at this moment, but that doesn't make you a failure. Let's take into consideration the following example. How many quarters does a basketball game have? Okay, four. If you and I are playing basketball and in the first quarter my score is 18 and yours is 20, who is winning? You! If in the second quarter my score is 22 and yours is 25, who is winning? You! But have I lost? It may seem as if I am going to lose, but have you ever heard of a comeback? You see, there is a difference between losing and lost. You cannot have a comeback without a setback. You cannot have a testimony without a test. The sweetest victory comes after the heaviest battle.

I will never forget the game between the Buffalo Bills and Houston Oilers in 1993. I remember staring at the television in awe as the Buffalo Bills were led into victory by their backup quarterback. The term "backup" means that he would only play in the event of an injury. This moment has been marked in history as the greatest comeback in the NFL. The Bills were losing terribly. In fact, the score was so bad that by mid-game the Bills fans began to leave. They were certain their team was going to lose. Apparently the backup quarterback did not receive the memo that the game was lost. With the mindset of a champion, he helped turn the entire game around bringing the score to 38-35 with only three minutes left in the game. Eventually the Bills won, concluding the largest comeback victory (32 points) in NFL history.

The Bills were losing, but the backup quarterback was able to redeem them and lead them into victory. Many times we feel as though because we are losing, all is lost. The score may not always look good. Some may even give up on you. Even though you are losing, know that there is a comeback in you. You cannot have a comeback if you were never behind. There will be times when you are behind. Embrace this and then bounce back. Are you in pursuit of that which you are called to do, or have you given up? When the odds may not be in your favor, when others have given up on you, no matter what the score is, as long as there is still time in the game, there is a comeback in you. So catapult yourself, catch up, and prepare for your comeback.

Discouragement and Rejection

Do you remember the first time you decided to apply for a job opening? You probably felt incredible. You may have had full confidence that you were able to perform the tasks required for the job. How about the first time you launched your business? You were completely assured that you could outperform any competition if given a chance. You set forth your proposal, waited, and then someone slammed a door in your face. Shortly after this, you received another rejection, and then another followed soon after. Does this experience sound familiar? How did you react? Maybe your confidence was affected by the rejections.

Have you ever observed the way people react to rejection? Some become paralyzed and never try again while others use it to power an unstoppable attitude of unrelenting persistence. Becoming paralyzed by discouragement and rejection is common, and the consequences can be deadly to your mission. Discouragement and rejection are real, but don't let these feelings cause you to stop pursuing your goal. Don't allow rejection to destroy you, even when it makes you feel incapable. Rejection terminates your confidence and self-assurance, making you feel inadequate. You owe it to yourself to fight beyond the struggle that rejection often brings. It is inevitable that you will experience rejection, but how will you respond to it? Will you break down the barriers and push beyond the lethal dose of discouragement rejection administers? Will you allow it to depress you and cause you to give up? Your goal depends on your ability to get back up after rejection pushes you down. The way you choose to react to rejection could determine whether you will achieve your goal. It could determine whether you will keep applying for that job position you so badly want. It could determine whether you will hit your sales target this month. It could determine whether you will hit your savings goal. High achievers and risk takers don't care about rejection. They realize that it is part of the journey. High achievers continue forward and onward to find the solution that will bring the results they desire. Expect to be rejected. This is part of the journey. Embrace it.

I would like to add that rejection isn't always the end. For example, although someone may reject you now, later they may give you the sale. Think of it as a seed planted. A potential client may not be ready to do business with you at the time you approached them, but they may do business with you at a later date. Don't let the rejection be a defining moment for you. Also, examine the criticism and learn from it. There may be some truth to what your critics are saying. Use this and apply it to make yourself better. Use it as a method to improve.

Realize that you are not the sum of the denials you are experiencing. Rather, you are the sum of your hard work, skills, and persistence that have brought you this far. If you doubt your worth the moment someone tells you no, then you may never achieve your goals. Remember, results matter, not the opinions of others. Your value lies in the results you bring to the table. Embrace your individuality and continue to rise up. Take a stand against the opinions of others. When it gets tough, be your own cheerleader and keep moving forward, no matter how bad it looks.

There is a significant cost attached to giving up. Are you prepared to deal with that? Are you prepared to deal with wasted resources, unused talent, and an unfulfilled purpose? Rejection and setbacks are often a test of life to see how determined you are to achieve your goal. You must remain level headed, confident, and in pursuit of your goal. You must embrace the journey of its achievement. A journey is most times far from perfect. It is usually filled with potholes, trials, and challenging encounters. However, at the end of most journeys, we grow. We develop a shell that encompasses us and make us resilient. How many times have you risen up from the ashes of a situation stronger than before? The moment you quit, every rejection directed at you is validated, every radical move wasted, and every fundamental experience squandered. Keep going. Push past each rejection until you reach the "yes" life has to offer.

"An excellent and diligent performance will often lead to excellent and dynamic results."

CHAPTER FIVE

Results

(Belief, Vision, Attitude) + (Performance) = (Results)

Faith + Works = Success

So, you've given your best performance, and now you are achieving tremendous results because of it. An excellent and diligent performance will often lead to excellent and dynamic results. Results speak to the effective outcome of your hard work. Maybe you got that promotion you applied for. Perhaps you've achieved your savings goal. You may have graduated with honors from medical school. Whatever it is, I'm sure the process of overcoming the challenges and obstacles you faced was worth it.

The formula provided by this book operates very much the way the body works together. All parts of the formula are important and crucial when accomplishing a goal. For example, if you see a beggar, your first instinct may be to give him some money. First, your heart feels compassion for him. Next, your heart tells your head what it is you want to do. Your head may think about it and consider the right amount to give. Last, your hand takes the money and gives it to the beggar. Your heart, head, and hand worked together to achieve this goal.

Belief, vision, attitude, and performance all work together to bring about successful results. Belief, vision, and attitude are all abstract. These three embody your heart and mindset. Performance represents work. This embodies execution. Align these four together, and you will achieve the desired results. As stated in the previous chapter, faith plus works brings success. Just as the heart, head, and hand work together to bring about success, so must belief, vision, attitude, and performance work together to bring about the desired results. Each principle in the *Maximum Me* formula sets you up to propel you into the next.

The body working in its perfect function is successful. The head speaks to how you think. This is your attitude, your intellect, doing whatever it takes. Do what you have to do. You may not have it figured out in your head, but you will feel it in your heart. Your heart speaks to your belief system. This is your passion. Your hand speaks to your performance. In the ancient biblical scrolls, the hand is represented as work. It represents execution. When your heart, head, and hand are in perfect alignment, your body functions properly. Don't try to compare which is more important because all are needed to work together in order to function as a unit. Just as the hand needs the head and the head needs the heart, each function in the model I have shown you all need each other in order to bring about success. Let your heart, head, and hand work together, and the objective you have set out to achieve will more than likely come. If you believe, plan and prepare, you can achieve your dreams.

Vision needs belief to be generated in order to stimulate an "I will do whatever it takes" attitude. In order for an exceptional execution to take place, performance needs attitude. In order to achieve dynamic results, a good performance is needed. Each part of the formula is deliberately aligned to achieve success. This formula gives you a powerful edge when achieving your goals. It is my hope that when you apply this formula, you will indeed see that you can achieve your desired goals.

After you have achieved dynamic results, make room for

- Celebration
- Appreciation
- Gratitude
- Thank You

Celebrating your results is important. Acknowledging you and your team's hard work and recognizing monumental moments at the end of a journey will give you the sense of value you'll need for your next venture. It boosts your confidence and assures you of your abilities. It reminds you that you are capable of achieving the success you set out to accomplish. Your results can boost your credibility and demand the respect you deserve. Whether you are celebrating with dinner or a press release, celebrating helps you to realize how far you've come and the hurdles you have gone over to achieve your goal. It recognizes your growth.

Appreciate how far you've come. Appreciate the hard work and consistent action that led to your results. Realize your journey was worth it. The rejections that pointed you in the direction of your "yes" were worth it. Your journey is an experience that increases your value as an individual. With your experience comes a new set of knowledge, skills, and capabilities. Your portfolio is now strengthened. You can use this experience to give rise to other undertakings and endeavors. A student who just received his degree in business management may apply for a position within a private firm or start his own business. An individual who achieved her savings goal may coach others on how they too can achieve their savings goal. Your experience now opens doors for more opportunities. It makes room for new possibilities. It is valuable and you will be able to capitalize on it. Knowledge is power. Making the most of your experience benefits you and can even benefit others who desire to walk the same path as you.

Be grateful for your journey. Gratitude helps to keep you humble. Delight in your achievements, and enjoy the results of your hard work. Many people work long, diligent hours and never truly enjoy the satisfaction their results bring with it. Take that vacation in Hawaii. Visit the spa. Take a tour of London. Treat yourself to dinner at a five-star restaurant. Purchase that bottle of perfume. Your hard work deserves to be rewarded. Your consistent commitment to succeeding has paid off. Also, when you have completed your journey, pay it forward. Help someone else in their journey, even if it is just an encouraging word.

Remember to say thank you to those who have helped you along the way. Your journey would not have been successful without the help of others. Someone helped you along the way. Someone may have given you guidance, a kind word, or even a scholarship. Whether it is a high school teacher or an old boss, someone supported you during your voyage. Recognizing and acknowledging people who supported you shows that you have identified their value and are grateful. Few remember to say thank you.

In the book of Luke, we are told of Jesus healing ten lepers. Of these ten lepers only one remembered to say thank you. One leper returned and expressed his gratitude to Jesus. Jesus asked "Were not ten lepers healed? Where are the others?" The Bible tell us that Jesus replied, "Rise and go; your faith has made you well." Remembering to say thank you is significant. It reminds those mentors and all who assisted you along your journey that they are appreciated for the pivotal role they played in the life of someone else. This is special and unique and should be celebrated. Recognize these individuals and give them credit for their influence, even if you don't consider it to be big.

I ran into Bagsy two decades after receiving his advice. At the time, I had long achieved the goal of branch manager he had hoped for me to achieve and was now the Senior Manager at the bank. I was returning from having lunch with my Vice President and some of my colleagues. We had stopped for lunch at the foot of the Paradise Island bridge to grab a quick bite. I looked across the street, and just at the entrance of the dock, I saw a group of men lying around, hanging out, and heavily drinking. Bagsy was one of them! He recognized me. In fact, Bagsy saw me before I saw him.

I later learned that at this moment he was telling his drinking buddies, "I know him!"

Their response was "Yeah, right!" They did not believe him. "How could *you* know him?" they wondered.

Bagsy kept insisting, "That's the bank manager! I know him!"

What happened next amazed everyone. He waved at me from afar, and I waved back! His reaction was priceless. As I approached him, his smile got even wider. He grinned excitedly. His buddies began to look at him as if to say, "*You* know somebody?" My work colleagues must have thought I had lost my mind. I went over regardless, and this confirmed exactly what Bagsy was trying to tell his buddies. He lit up the moment I came over.

"Ricky," he said. "I was telling them that I know you!"

I looked at them and said, "Listen, this man here saved my business career because he gave me excellent advice!" As I spoke, Bagsy was beaming with pride and appreciated my recognition of him. What I saw in Bagsy's face was priceless.

His friends looked at him in disbelief. They were amazed! They looked at Bagsy as if to say, "*You* were a positive influence on somebody?"

Bagsy told them of my story and how I was the talk of Seagrape, Grand Bahama. I stood beside Bagsy as he told my story of being the town hero. I made sure they knew that I may have been the town hero, but Bagsy was in fact the real hero.

My colleagues were extremely shocked, but when I came back and explained why I went over to Bagsy, they were all in awe.

They said to me, "We would have done the same. You had to go over there!"

I have only seen Bagsy a few times, but when I do, there is always a powerful exchange.

It is important to recognize those people who helped you along the way. Someone did something or said something along the way that helped you on your journey. It may have been a teacher, a boss, or even your very own Bagsy. Recognize that person who helped you, and then pay it forward and invest in someone else. You may not be able to pay it forward monetarily, but a genuine thank you and a public recognition will go a long way. The look on Bagsy's face when I recognized him in front of his peers is proof of this.

No man is an island. You did not become successful by yourself. The most selfish term I have ever heard is the phrase "self-made millionaire." You did not accomplish it all on your own. Take the time to appreciate those who helped raise you to the level you are. At some point, someone saw something in you that helped you. What Bagsy saw in me, in a sense, embodies this book's message. He believed in my ability, and through that unforgettable exchange, he helped me to see the vision of what was possible if I possessed the right attitude. This led to me making every effort to perform at the highest level consistently which led to my success. Although I am still growing and learning, Bagsy's belief has helped me to become the best version of me today — the maximum me.

Sources and Citations

https://www.bahamasolympiccommittee.org/legends

King James Version (KJV)

Congratulations, you have completed the journey of Maximum Me. I hope this formula will impact the voyage that lies before you in a positive way. May it assist you in becoming the most powerful version of you. The most powerful version of you requires hard work and dedication. When aligned correctly, belief, vision, attitude, and performance are extremely effective. This unique formula enables you to achieve dynamic results almost every time. Through hard work and determination, you can achieve outstanding results. The climb will be tough; however, you must keep climbing. There will be challenges; however, you must remain faithful. Don't allow discouragement and rejection to cause you to stop. Keep pushing. Remember, life was designed to say "yes" to all of your dreams.

May you become the most powerful version of you — the maximum you.

Maximum Me Inc.

Maximum Me Inc. was founded by Maxwell R. Jones. It is a platform committed to helping individuals and organizations to take action and achieve profound results in the areas of both life and business. Our mission is to empower individuals to rise as leaders and take charge of their destiny through hard work and deliberate measures. Through books, courses, one-on-one coaching, group and corporate training, Maximum Me Inc. delivers content that equips individuals and organizations to meet and in most cases exceed expectations. Our content assists in giving you the competitive edge you need to become the most powerful version of you — the maximum you.

About the Author

Maxwell R. Jones lives in The Bahamas. He grew up in the settlement of Sea Grape in Eight Mile Rock, Grand Bahama. He is the son of Johnny and Bernice Jones — a taxi driver and straw vendor. Being the product of this unique combination has contributed significantly to who he is today. He is a proud husband, loving father, and the founder of the motivational and training company Maximum Me Inc. His extraordinary speaking ability has enabled him to grace many stages both live and virtual, in the Caribbean, the United States of America, and Canada. In addition, he is a songwriter and enjoys writing poetry. His company offers a wide range of services including training on the topics of providing excellent customer service, sales, and motivating corporations and individuals to take action and improve performance. He respectfully holds an executive position at the largest Bahamian owned bank in The Bahamas. He has been in the banking arena for over three decades and has worked his way up the ranks through hard work and dedication. Maxwell Jones encourages individuals to tap into their full potential by digging deep when pursuing their dreams and goals.

Maximum Me Inc.

The Maximum Me Inc. team remains dedicated to helping you to become the most powerful version of you. Feel free to contact us if you are interested in advancing your growth with us. Allow us to continue to help guide you as we provide the following facilities:

Private Coaching

Embrace your full potential with our one-on-one intensives.

Group Coaching

Take your organization to the next level with our group coaching package.

Corporate Training

Give your executive team the competitve edge they need to help propel them into their most powerful year with our leadership, finance, growth strategy, customer service, and sales training opportunities.

Email maxwellrjones1@gmail.com if you or your organization would like to further develop and accelerate your potential with Maximum Me Inc.

https://www.facebook.com/Maximum-Me-Maxwell-R-Jones-1081469058714656

Made in the USA
Middletown, DE
27 May 2021